Most Remarkable American Entrepreneurs

Frederick Koh

Series Editor
Jeffrey D. Wilhelm

Much thought, debate, and research went into choosing and ranking the 10 items in each book in this series. We realize that everyone has his or her own opinion of what is most significant, revolutionary, amazing, deadly, and so on. As you read, you may agree with our choices, or you may be surprised — and that's the way it should be!

an imprint of

SCHOLASTIC

www.scholastic.com/librarypublishing

A Rubicon book published in association with Scholastic Inc.

 © 2008 Rubicon Publishing Inc.
www.rubiconpublishing.com

All rights reserved. No part of this publication may be reproduced, stored in a database or retrieval system, distributed, or transmitted in any form or by any means, electronic, mechanical, photocopying, recording, or otherwise, without the prior written permission of Rubicon Publishing Inc.

 is a trademark of The 10 Books

SCHOLASTIC and associated logos and designs are trademarks and/or registered trademarks of Scholastic Inc.

Associate Publishers: Kim Koh, Miriam Bardswich
Project Editor: Amy Land
Editors: Elizabeth Siegel, Christine Boocock
Creative Director: Jennifer Drew
Project Manager/Designer: Jeanette MacLean
Graphic Designers: Julie Whatman, Rebecca Buchanan, Brandon Köpke, Sherwin Flores

The publisher gratefully acknowledges the following for permission to reprint copyrighted material in this book.

Every reasonable effort has been made to trace the owners of copyrighted material and to make due acknowledgment. Any errors or omissions drawn to our attention will be gladly rectified in future editions.

"America's Inventive Entrepreneur" (excerpt) from "The Entrepreneurial Leadership of Thomas Edison: America's Inventive Colossus," by James Watkinson and *Insight* staff. Reprinted with permission of *Babson Insight*.

Cover Image: Oprah Winfrey–Photo by Soren McCarty/WireImage/Getty Images

Library and Archives Canada Cataloguing in Publication

Koh, Frederick
    The 10 most remarkable American entrepreneurs / Frederick Koh.

Includes index.
ISBN: 978-1-55448-498-0

    1. Readers (Elementary). 2. Readers—Businesspeople.
I. Title. II. Title: Ten most remarkable American entrepreneurs.

PE1117.K655 2007   428.6   C2007-906917-7

1 2 3 4 5 6 7 8 9 10   10   17 16 15 14 13 12 11 10 09 08

Printed in Singapore

Contents

Introduction: Big Ideas 4

Madam Walker 6
It took more than just hard work for Walker to become one of the wealthiest self-made entrepreneurs of the early 20th century.

P. T. Barnum 10
From sideshows to circuses, this showbiz genius made his mark on the entertainment business.

Mary Kay Ash 14
Mary Kay Ash was much more than pink Cadillacs and cosmetics — she was a winner all the way!

Sergey Brin and Larry Page 18
They are the brains behind the world's most popular online search engine.

Sam Walton 22
Chances are you've heard of Wal-Mart — Sam Walton's global retail chain.

Oprah Winfrey 26
This enterprising American icon is more than just a talk-show host.

Ray Kroc 30
The iconic "golden arches" might not be so famous if this visionary hadn't been in charge.

Bill Gates 34
He revolutionized the computer industry and the way we work and play.

Henry Ford 38
This innovative entrepreneur ushered in the modern era of transportation and changed our way of life.

Thomas Edison 42
A creative and scientific genius, Edison's impressive inventions became big business.

We Thought … 46
What Do You Think? 47
Index 48

Big IDEAS

What are your plans for the future? Do you hope to find a job? Or have you dreamed of starting a business?

Entrepreneurs are people who are prepared to take risks and work hard to turn their ideas into successful businesses. There are no guarantees of success. But for those who make it, success brings personal wealth, recognition, and influence.

In this book, we present the people we think are the 10 most remarkable entrepreneurs in the United States. These are individuals with vision, drive, and determination. Strong leaders and risk takers, these entrepreneurs know how to spot opportunities and make the most of them.

In ranking these entrepreneurs, we considered the following criteria: What obstacles did the entrepreneur overcome to make it to the top? Did the entrepreneur create a groundbreaking product or conduct business in an *innovative* way? What impact did the business have on Americans and on people around the world? What did the entrepreneur give back to the community? What is the size of the entrepreneur's business?

As you read about these amazing people, consider the significance of their achievements. Ask yourself:

---

innovative: creative; having original ideas

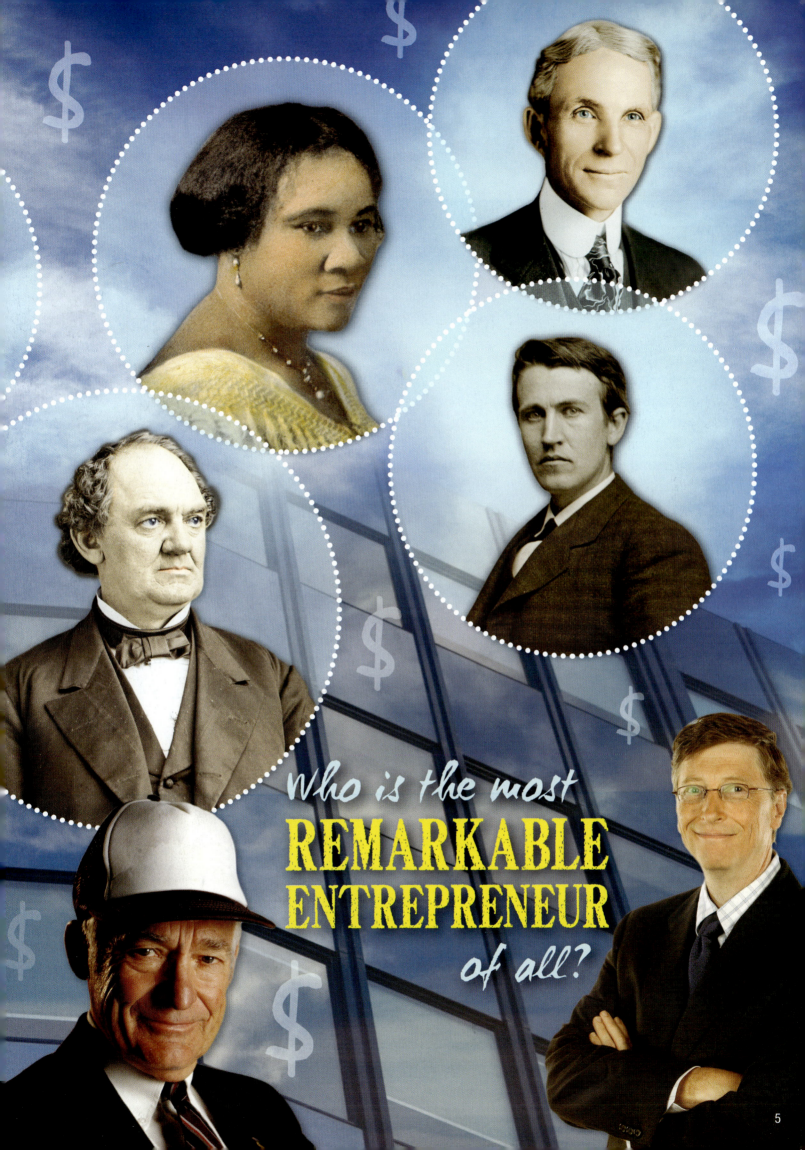

10 MADAM WALK

Before becoming a successful entrepreneur, Sarah Breedlove worked as a cotton picker, a washerwoman, a cook, and a sales agent.

BIO: 1867–1919. Born Sarah Breedlove in Delta, Louisiana; changed her name to Madam C. J. Walker; went into business in her late 30s

THE BUSINESS: Developed and sold her own line of hair-care products for African-American women

> "There is no royal flower-strewn path to success. And if there is, I have not found it — for if I have accomplished anything in life it is because I have been willing to work hard."
> — MADAM C. J. WALKER

Sarah Breedlove was the daughter of formerly enslaved African-American parents. She did what was unthinkable for a woman in the late 19th century — she started her own business.

Breedlove started her business in 1905 after discovering a formula to treat her own hair loss from a scalp ailment. She prepared her formula at home and began selling it door to door. In 1906, she moved to Denver where she met her second husband, Charles Joseph Walker, a newspaperman. She adopted his name and called herself Madam C. J. Walker.

Madam Walker advertised and promoted her hair formula. She convinced other African-American women to sell her hair-care product. Sales grew, allowing her to set up a factory in Pittsburgh to produce other hair-care products such as shampoos, conditioners, and gels. She also opened a school to give professional training to her salespeople. By the time of her death, Madam Walker had trained some 40,000 women. With annual sales of $500,000, her company became one of the largest businesses owned by an African American. Madam Walker became one of the wealthiest African-American women of her time.

ailment: *disease or disorder*

MADAM WALKER

GETTING THERE

Orphaned at age seven, Madam Walker worked for many years in the cotton fields. At 14, she married and had a child. When her husband died four years later, she went to work as a washerwoman for $1.50 a week to support herself and her child. In the 1890s, Madam Walker temporarily lost her hair. She experimented with different treatments for her problem. In the process, she came up with a formula that worked. In 1906, she quit her job and started her own business.

THE RIGHT STUFF

It took great courage for an African-American woman to go into business in a male-dominated society. In the beginning, Madam Walker took a part-time job to support herself and her business. She was confident her business would succeed, and she worked hard at it. She convinced other African-American women to join her sales team. Her message to them was, "I did it from nothing, you can do it, too." She started a school to provide sales training to her team.

? What do you think might have been the most difficult challenge for Madam Walker on her road to success?

GIVING BACK

Madam Walker's achievements went beyond business success. She was one of America's first African-American philanthropists. She used her wealth and connections to make a difference. She donated large sums of money to African-American causes. These included the YMCA and the National Association for the Advancement of Colored People (NAACP).

philanthropists: *people who donate large amounts of money, often to charity*

Quick Fact
Madam Walker encouraged her employees to give to charity, saying, "I want you to understand that your first duty is to humanity."

The Expert Says...

"She had an indomitable spirit that prevailed through the difficulties of finding capital and through the difficulties of her own very limited social position. In a market in which there weren't many realms where women could play, she found a way."

— Nancy F. Koehn, Harvard Business School

indomitable: *strong and stubborn*
capital: *money used to start or build a business*

Madam Walker's first product was the popular Madam C.J. Walker's Wonderful Hair Grower.

10

Leading The Way

Madam C. J. Walker overcame incredible odds and became a successful entrepreneur. This report documents her legacy.

Humble Beginnings

"I am a woman who came from the cotton fields of the South. I was promoted from there to the washtub. Then I was promoted to the cook kitchen. And from there I promoted myself into the business of manufacturing hair goods and preparations. ... I have built my own factory on my own ground."
— Madam C. J. Walker, speaking at the National Negro Business League Convention, 1912

A'Lelia, Madam C. J. Walker's daughter, gets a manicure. Her mother encouraged women to enter the hair-care and beauty business.

Sound Advice

Madam Walker believed in honest business dealings and quality products. Success came to her through hard work, perseverance, and a strong belief in herself.

Legacy

After her death in 1919, Madam Walker's daughter A'Lelia took over the business. By 1927, the business had grown even bigger. A'Lelia built the Madam C.J. Walker Building in Indianapolis in 1928. It was the national headquarters and the manufacturing plant of the Madam C. J. Walker Manufacturing Company. It was also a social and cultural center for African Americans. Today, the Walker Building is a historic landmark.

In 1998, Madam Walker became the 21st African American to be featured in the United States Postal Service's Black Heritage Series. This enterprising woman's life is described in the biography, *On Her Own Ground: The Life and Times of Madam C. J. Walker*.

Quick Fact

Madam C. J. Walker is listed in the *Guinness Book of World Records* as the first self-made female African-American millionaire.

Take Note

Madam Walker takes the #10 spot. She did what few women of her time would even dream of doing. She took a big risk by going into business, and she succeeded in a big way. She was an inspiration for other African-American women.
- Think about what Nancy F. Koehn says of Madam Walker. How would you describe this remarkable entrepreneur if you were to introduce her to a group of businesspeople?

⑨ P.T. BARNUM

P. T. Barnum, seen here in 1860, revolutionized the entertainment business.

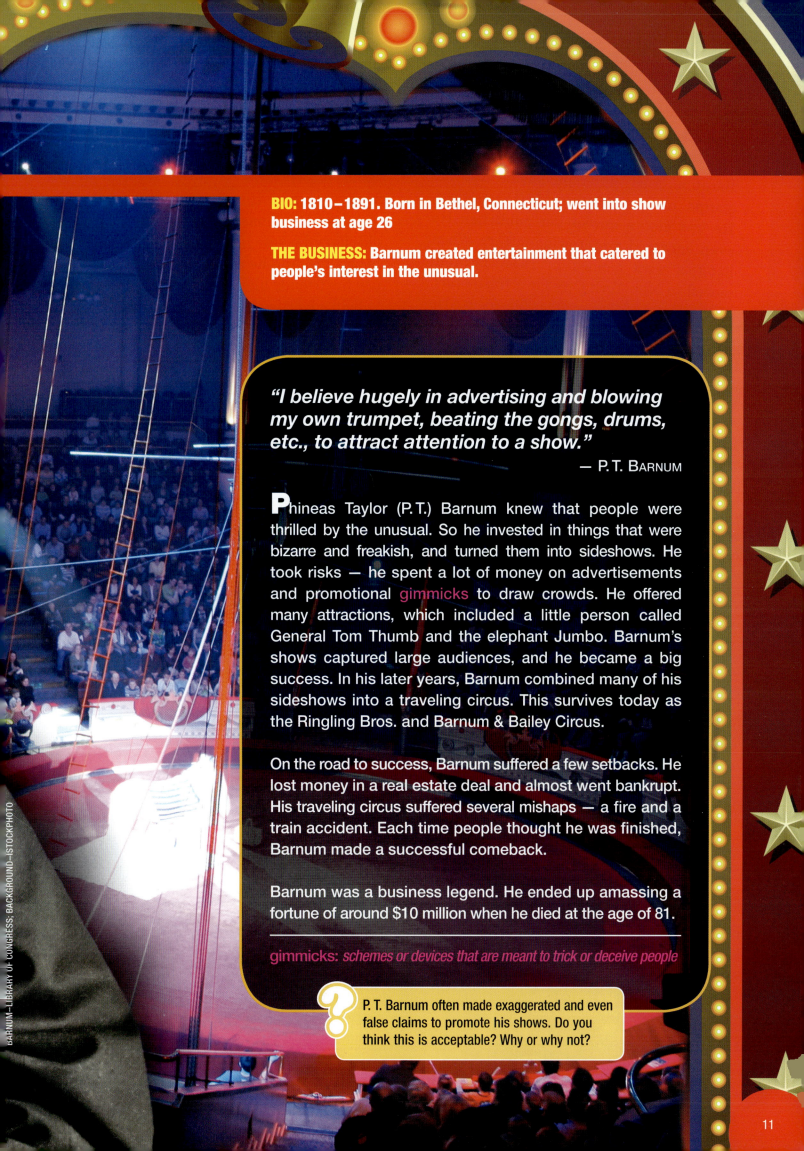

BIO: 1810–1891. Born in Bethel, Connecticut; went into show business at age 26

THE BUSINESS: Barnum created entertainment that catered to people's interest in the unusual.

> *"I believe hugely in advertising and blowing my own trumpet, beating the gongs, drums, etc., to attract attention to a show."*
> — P. T. Barnum

Phineas Taylor (P. T.) Barnum knew that people were thrilled by the unusual. So he invested in things that were bizarre and freakish, and turned them into sideshows. He took risks — he spent a lot of money on advertisements and promotional gimmicks to draw crowds. He offered many attractions, which included a little person called General Tom Thumb and the elephant Jumbo. Barnum's shows captured large audiences, and he became a big success. In his later years, Barnum combined many of his sideshows into a traveling circus. This survives today as the Ringling Bros. and Barnum & Bailey Circus.

On the road to success, Barnum suffered a few setbacks. He lost money in a real estate deal and almost went bankrupt. His traveling circus suffered several mishaps — a fire and a train accident. Each time people thought he was finished, Barnum made a successful comeback.

Barnum was a business legend. He ended up amassing a fortune of around $10 million when he died at the age of 81.

gimmicks: *schemes or devices that are meant to trick or deceive people*

? P. T. Barnum often made exaggerated and even false claims to promote his shows. Do you think this is acceptable? Why or why not?

P.T. BARNUM

GETTING THERE

Barnum tried different businesses. He started as a storekeeper in Connecticut. He was also a newspaper publisher. He even operated a statewide lottery. When lotteries were banned in 1834, Barnum moved to New York City for a fresh start. He explored different showbiz ideas. He purchased a museum and renamed it "Barnum's American Museum." To attract attention, he added a huge lighthouse lamp, put up flags, and placed exhibits of stuffed animals, giants, little people, jugglers, and models of cities on the museum's roof. The museum was a hit. It received 40 million visitors during Barnum's lifetime.

THE RIGHT STUFF

Barnum recognized that people are naturally curious. He was always looking out for unusual things to showcase. He once paid $1,000 to a blind, elderly, and paralyzed woman in New York City and turned her into a successful sideshow. He claimed the woman was 161 years old. Barnum saw nothing wrong in puffing up his claims. And he didn't think it was wrong to use his friends and connections in high places to help advertise his businesses.

Quick Fact
Barnum became active in politics. He was elected to the Connecticut legislature, and he served as mayor of Bridgeport, Connecticut, in 1875 and 1876.

? The Ringling Bros. and Barnum & Bailey Circus still exists today. What are the appeals of a circus?

GIVING BACK

Barnum was a generous supporter of the Universalist Society in Bridgeport. He gave close to $200,000 to the society to fund several colleges. In addition, Barnum donated money to the Woman's Centenary Association and helped to start Bridgeport Hospital in 1878. He was the hospital's first president.

A Barnum & Bailey poster of a bearded lady from about 1900

The Expert Says...

" The public wanted what Barnum had to offer: unusual entertainment. Barnum used **outlandish** stunts and curiosities to call attention to his show. But once he had people in his door, he satisfied them. "

— Joe Vitale, author of *There's a Customer Born Every Minute: P.T. Barnum's Secrets to Business Success*

outlandish: *bizarre; weird*

"THE PRINCE OF HUMBUG"

Barnum was sometimes less than truthful in his advertising. In 1842, he announced that he was displaying the remains of a real mermaid. In reality, it was the upper body of an ape that had been stitched onto the lower body of a fish. This, and other instances of stretching the truth, are shown in the following quotations from Barnum's book *The Autobiography of P.T. Barnum: Clerk, Merchant, Editor, and Showman*.

> As a businessman, my prime object has been to put money in my purse. I succeeded beyond my ... anticipations ... [But I have also] been a public benefactor, seldom paralleled. ...

> My traveling museums of natural history have been the largest and most interesting ever exhibited in the United States. ... No author or university even, has ever accomplished as much in the diffusion of knowledge ... of animal life.

> I have advertised my curiosities and my artists with all the ingenuity of which I was capable. ... No one, however, for himself can say that he ever paid for admission to one of my exhibitions more than his admission was worth to him.

paralleled: *equaled or matched*
diffusion: *spreading*
ingenuity: *skillful or brilliant in ideas; resourceful*

Quick Fact
Barnum had great partners in his circus business. One of them pioneered the use of railway cars to move the circus from town to town. Another partner, James A. Bailey, turned the circus into a popular show and sold it to the Ringling brothers in 1907.

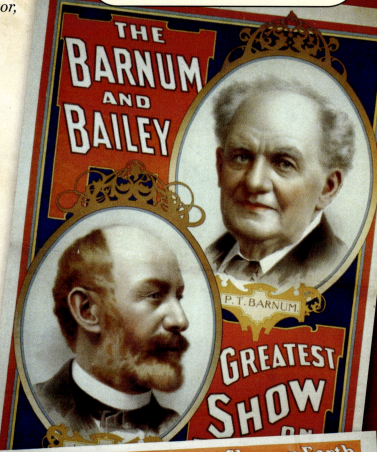

Take Note
P. T. Barnum takes center stage at #9. He broke new ground in the entertainment business and was one of the greatest showbiz personalities of all times. He was a remarkable entrepreneur, never afraid to risk his money or reputation. He also gave generously to the causes he supported.
- Do you think P. T. Barnum belongs in a book featuring remarkable entrepreneurs? Give reasons to support your answer.

8 MARY KAY ASH

Mary Kay Ash, seen here in 1981, began her business in 1963 at the age of 45.

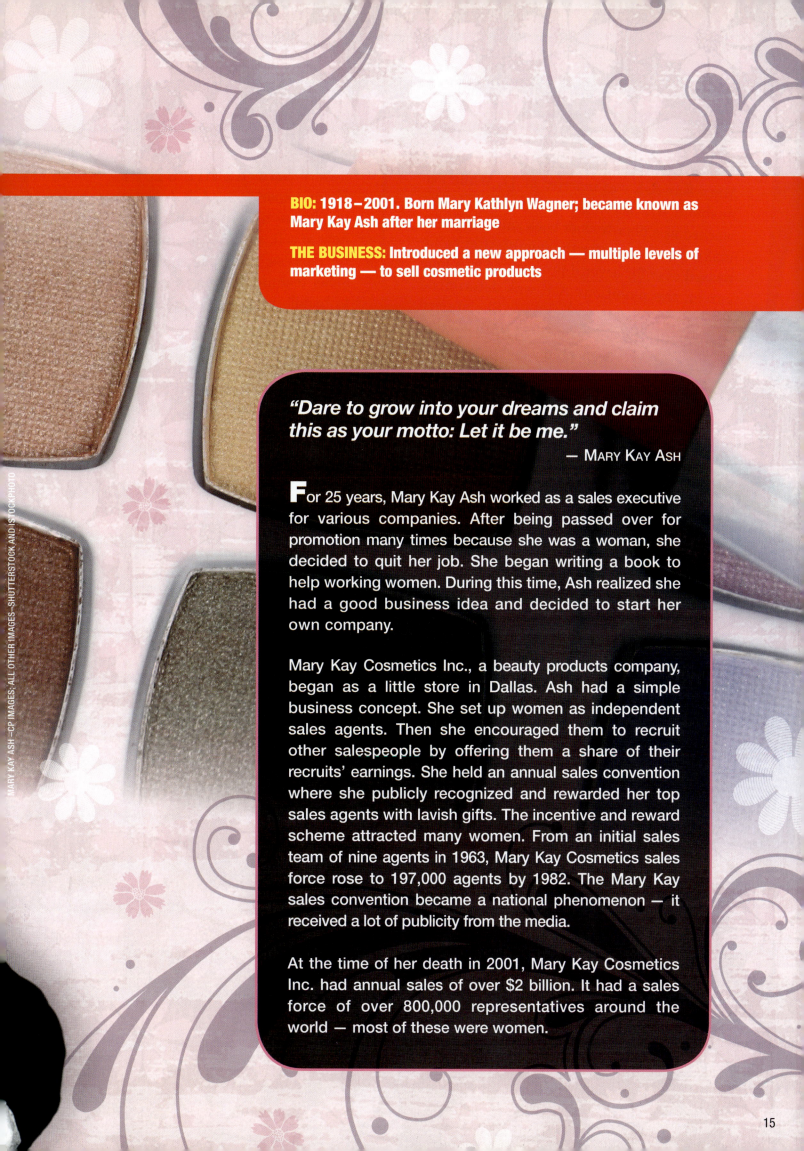

BIO: 1918–2001. Born Mary Kathlyn Wagner; became known as Mary Kay Ash after her marriage

THE BUSINESS: Introduced a new approach — multiple levels of marketing — to sell cosmetic products

"Dare to grow into your dreams and claim this as your motto: Let it be me."

— Mary Kay Ash

For 25 years, Mary Kay Ash worked as a sales executive for various companies. After being passed over for promotion many times because she was a woman, she decided to quit her job. She began writing a book to help working women. During this time, Ash realized she had a good business idea and decided to start her own company.

Mary Kay Cosmetics Inc., a beauty products company, began as a little store in Dallas. Ash had a simple business concept. She set up women as independent sales agents. Then she encouraged them to recruit other salespeople by offering them a share of their recruits' earnings. She held an annual sales convention where she publicly recognized and rewarded her top sales agents with lavish gifts. The incentive and reward scheme attracted many women. From an initial sales team of nine agents in 1963, Mary Kay Cosmetics sales force rose to 197,000 agents by 1982. The Mary Kay sales convention became a national phenomenon — it received a lot of publicity from the media.

At the time of her death in 2001, Mary Kay Cosmetics Inc. had annual sales of over $2 billion. It had a sales force of over 800,000 representatives around the world — most of these were women.

MARY KAY ASH

GETTING THERE

Mary Kay Ash was married at 17. While her husband was serving in World War II, she worked as a door-to-door book salesperson to make extra money for the family. After being passed over for several promotions in a long career, the ambitious Ash was determined to achieve success on her own. She started a cosmetics business in 1963 with $5,000, and recruited salespeople who were mainly women. Mary Kay allowed her salespeople to create their own work schedules. This helped them balance work and family life.

 What can you learn from Ash about starting up a business?

Quick Fact

Ash wrote several books. Her book *Mary Kay on People Management* was required reading at Harvard Business School. Her autobiographies *Mary Kay: The Story of America's Most Dynamic Businesswoman* and *Mary Kay: You Can Have It All* were also best sellers.

THE RIGHT STUFF

From experience, Ash knew that her employees and agents had to be taught how to sell, and they should be rewarded for success. She gave them training in sales techniques and taught them how to handle rejection and setbacks. A good communicator, Ash spoke to her sales teams regularly, and motivated them with stories of achievements. She was most creative in using the annual Mary Kay convention as a venue to give her staff public recognition and to promote her business.

GIVING BACK

Mary Kay started the Mary Kay Ash Charitable Foundation in 1996. This non-profit organization funds research on cancers affecting women. It also promotes an end to violence against women.

 What are some factors you would consider before supporting a charity?

The Expert Says...

> So few people of her generation provided much real leadership in business — [Mary Kay] did. She used it to build a corporation that helped thousands of women build their own businesses and to be an inspiration for millions of people.

— John P. Kotter, professor at Harvard Business School

The Pink Cadillac

Mary Kay Ash motivated her sales team with gifts such as television sets, diamond bracelets, and holiday trips. But she was most remembered for the pink Cadillac. This **report** describes the story of this reward.

Mary Kay Ash is seen here with one of her trademark pink Cadillacs, in 1978.

In 1968, Mary Kay Ash ordered herself a Cadillac from General Motors. She had it custom painted in pink to match her Mary Kay makeup compact. The car was an instant hit with her sales force. So in 1969, she decided to award pink Cadillacs to the top five salespersons at her annual sales convention.

Since then, giving pink Cadillacs as **incentives** has become a tradition. Over 100,000 of these cars have been given out to date! General Motors, the company that makes Cadillacs, has even reserved Ash's preferred color of pink paint solely for use on cars made for Mary Kay Cosmetics Inc. Today, a sales director with a team that sells at least $96,000 in cosmetics in a six-month period can qualify for a pink Cadillac. Winners can choose cash instead of the Cadillac but most still opt for the car. For many, it is the ultimate symbol of success.

incentives: *rewards given to motivate people*

? Would the possibility of being rewarded with a fancy car make you want to work for a company? Why or why not? Is there another reward that would appeal to you more?

Quick Fact
Mary Kay Ash and her company have won many awards. Ash was Lifetime Television's "Most Outstanding Woman in Business in the 20th Century." In 1998, her company was listed in *Fortune* magazine as one of the 100 best companies to work for.

Take Note
Mary Kay Ash speeds away with the #8 spot. She had a simple business approach that motivated her employees. She built her business into a big American corporation and turned her company into a household name.
- Mary Kay Ash made her fortune selling beauty products. Compare her techniques with Madam C. J. Walker's. Do you agree that Ash should be ranked higher than Walker? Explain.

5   4   3   2   1

7 SERGEY BRIN

> "I was never one of the crowd ... I like to maintain my independence."
> — SERGEY BRIN

The names Sergey Brin and Larry Page might not sound familiar, but you've probably heard of their business. These two remarkable entrepreneurs worked together to create the online search engine that we have come to know as Google. Their invention changed the way people around the world search for information. It gives Internet users easy access to millions of Web pages. Now millions use the Google search engine each day.

Brin and Page succeeded in a very unusual way. They developed the ideas behind the search engine as a college project. They placed their search engine online in 1996 without any expectations. Little by little, people started using it. As the search engine's popularity grew, all Brin wanted was to sell it and pay off his credit card debts. But there were no buyers. So he and Page decided to take time off from their studies to develop their project into a real business. In 1998, they named their search engine Google and established Google Inc. Google was an instant success! Within a year, it became one of the most popular online search engines.

In 2004, Brin and Page decided to sell the company's shares online. Google stocks were snatched up fast. Google's share prices went from $85 to around $700 at the end of 2007. At that time, Brin and Page were estimated to be worth close to $20 billion each!

shares: *units of stock, or ownership, of a corporation*

 Brin and Page worked as a team to win the #7 spot. Who do you admire more, entrepreneurs who work as a team, or those who work alone? Why?

AND LARRY PAGE

BIO: Brin was born in Moscow in 1973; moved to the United States with his family when he was six. Page was born in 1973 in Michigan.

THE BUSINESS: An easy-to-use and effective online search engine; profits come from the sale of advertising space linked to keywords used in the search

Larry Page (left) and Sergey Brin

SERGEY BRIN AND LARRY PAGE

GETTING THERE

Sergey Brin met Larry Page, a fellow student at Stanford University, California, in 1995. They decided to jointly pursue their interest in finding better ways to categorize online information. Working tirelessly for many months, they came up with a way to rank and search Web sites using keywords and phrases. They wanted to sell their technology, but they did not have any offers. At the time, people used the World Wide Web mainly for emails. Internet companies did not see the relevance of online search.

Brin and Page then decided to take time off from their studies to develop their search engine into a business. They borrowed money from friends and individual investors to pay for rent and to buy computers. In less than two years, the Google guys became an extraordinary American success story.

THE RIGHT STUFF

Brin and Page made a winning team. They worked well together in managing the company. Page focused on product development, and Brin attended to the company's image and business. Today, Brin and Page continue to develop innovative products and online services. One of their groundbreaking products is Gmail, a free Web-based e-mail that can send, receive, and store large files. Google Earth is another amazing innovation. Its huge map of satellite and aerial photos allows users to zoom into any location on the globe. Brin and Page hire the best talents and create a unique work environment for their staff.

GIVING BACK

In 2005, Brin and Page created a non-profit organization called Google.org. It supports charities and companies that work on solutions to the problems of global poverty and environmental destruction. It is dedicated to increasing the usage of renewable energy. Brin and Page made a commitment to donate one percent of Google's profits to the foundation annually.

Google Inc. co-founders Sergey Brin (left) and Larry Page experiment with an electric hybrid car under a solar panel parking area at Google headquarters in Mountain View, California.

Quick Fact

In June 2006, the word Google was officially included as a verb in the *Oxford English Dictionary*. It means: "To search for information about (a person or thing) using the Google search engine."

The Expert Says…

" Not since Gutenberg invented the modern printing press more than 500 years ago … has any new invention empowered individuals or transformed access to information as profoundly as Google. "

— David Vise, Pulitzer Prize-winning journalist

Google: No. 1 Employer

Quick Fact
Google is a deliberate misspelling of Googol, which is a very big number in mathematics. It is the number equal to "1" followed by 100 zeros.

? Do you think it would have made a difference if the Google founders had gone with a different name for their search engine? Why or why not?

Many people say Google's success is due in part to how well it treats its employees. In 2007, it was listed as the "Best Company to Work for in America" by *Fortune* magazine. In fact, one of Google's slogans is "Work should be challenging and the challenge should be fun." This **photo essay** captures some of the benefits Google offers its employees.

Google promotes physical fitness as a way for employees to relax and recharge. Here, Google staffers take a break to play beach volleyball.

Google provides motorized scooters for employees to move around in Googleplex, or the Google headquarters.

In Google headquarters in Mountain View, California, employees don't have to worry about packing lunches. Google offers its employees free, delicious, healthy meals every day.

Take Note

These remarkably talented entrepreneurs earn the #7 ranking for their hugely successful business. Their innovative search engine has changed the lives of Americans and people around the world. And just think — both Brin and Page were in their twenties when they launched their business and achieved fame and fortune.
- Success came quickly to Sergey Brin and Larry Page. Does this make their accomplishment less impressive? Why or why not?

6 SAM WALTON

Walton's business, Wal-Mart, operates close to 7,000 stores in 15 countries around the world.

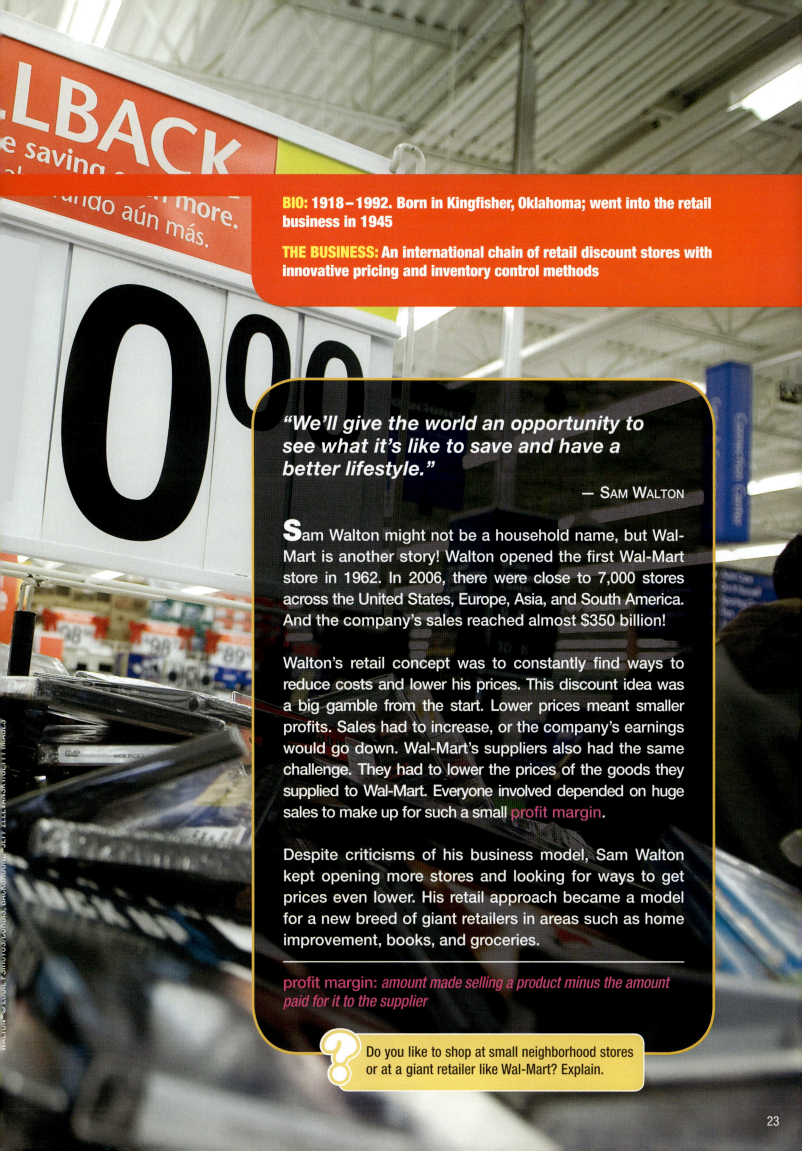

BIO: 1918–1992. Born in Kingfisher, Oklahoma; went into the retail business in 1945

THE BUSINESS: An international chain of retail discount stores with innovative pricing and inventory control methods

"We'll give the world an opportunity to see what it's like to save and have a better lifestyle."

— Sam Walton

Sam Walton might not be a household name, but Wal-Mart is another story! Walton opened the first Wal-Mart store in 1962. In 2006, there were close to 7,000 stores across the United States, Europe, Asia, and South America. And the company's sales reached almost $350 billion!

Walton's retail concept was to constantly find ways to reduce costs and lower his prices. This discount idea was a big gamble from the start. Lower prices meant smaller profits. Sales had to increase, or the company's earnings would go down. Wal-Mart's suppliers also had the same challenge. They had to lower the prices of the goods they supplied to Wal-Mart. Everyone involved depended on huge sales to make up for such a small profit margin.

Despite criticisms of his business model, Sam Walton kept opening more stores and looking for ways to get prices even lower. His retail approach became a model for a new breed of giant retailers in areas such as home improvement, books, and groceries.

profit margin: *amount made selling a product minus the amount paid for it to the supplier*

? Do you like to shop at small neighborhood stores or at a giant retailer like Wal-Mart? Explain.

SAM WALTON

GETTING THERE

Sam Walton went into the retail business in 1945. With $5,000 of his life's savings and a loan, he bought a variety store. The store's success led him to set up a small chain of variety stores called Walton's 5 & 10. Business was good, but Walton needed something special to deal with growing competition. In 1962, he opened the first Wal-Mart with its price-reducing concept.

> **Quick Fact**
> At the time of his death in 1992, Sam Walton was the second-richest person in America. Bill Gates was first.

> **Quick Fact**
> In 1998, *TIME* magazine listed Sam Walton among the "100 Most Influential People of the 20th Century."

THE RIGHT STUFF

Sam Walton excelled at school and in sports. He was smart and ambitious. As an entrepreneur, he had the vision to recognize that times were changing in the retail business. He was not afraid to gamble on his discount concept despite opposition from his suppliers. Walton was innovative. He kept his stores open later than other stores. He also introduced a profit-sharing scheme, giving part of the company's profits to staff in the form of cash or shares for their contribution to the company's success.

 Find out more about a profit-sharing scheme. What does it mean for the employer and employees?

GIVING BACK

Sam Walton supported many charitable causes, especially his church. In 1987, he started the Walton Family Foundation, which supports education and environmental conservation. It provides funds to economic projects that improve the quality of living in the Arkansas and Gulf regions of the United States. Walton left the foundation $172 million when he died in 1992. This amount has since grown to over $800 million.

In 1990, Sam Walton's first variety store was turned into the Wal-Mart Visitors Center. Located in Bentonville, Arkansas, the center is open to visitors eager to learn more about this American success story!

China's first Wal-Mart was opened in 1996 in Shenzhen. This ribbon-cutting ceremony was held to celebrate the opening.

> **The Expert Says…**
> "Wal-Mart brought low prices to small cities, but its creator also changed the way Big Business is run."
> — John Huey, Editor in Chief, TIME Inc.

Walton's World

Sam Walton turned one variety store into a global chain of discount centers. Today, Wal-Mart is popular in many countries around the world. Read these newspaper headlines to get a better understanding of Walton's impressive impact.

GHOST OF SAM WALTON:
An American Original
New Internationalist, July 2000

Sam Walton embodies the entrepreneurial spirit and epitomizes the American dream.

epitomizes: *is a typical example of*

10 Years Young — And Growing Up Quickly
DSN Retailing Today, June 2001

When the first Wal-Mart unit opened south of the border in November 1991 … it marked the beginning of the retailer's international expansion and the fulfillment of founder Sam Walton's vision to be a global company.

WAL-MART TOPS FORTUNE 500 LIST
Third straight year that retailer has topped U.S. companies
The Associated Press, March 2004

… With sales of almost $259 billion … the late Sam Walton's global chain of general stores topped the list of the nation's largest publicly-traded companies for the third straight year.

Quick Fact
David Glass, chief executive officer of Wal-Mart from 1988 to 2000, increased sales from $628 million to $5.4 billion, and the number of employees from 183,000 to over one million.

THE GREAT Wal-Mart Of China
Fortune magazine, July 2005

For the world's biggest company, the key to growth lies in the world's biggest country.

Take Note
Sam Walton takes the #6 spot on our list. As an entrepreneur, he was willing to take risks and challenge existing business models. He introduced new concepts to the retail business. He appreciated staff commitment and loyalty, and motivated his employees with profit-sharing incentives. He turned Wal-Mart into a global business empire.
- Do you agree that Sam Walton "epitomizes the American dream"? Give reasons to support your answer.

5 OPRAH WINF

Oprah Winfrey stops and talks to the media while fans gather behind her during her Live Your Best Life Tour at the Colorado Convention Center on April 30, 2005, in Denver.

REY

BIO: Born 1954 in rural Mississippi; became a reporter at 17; started her own production company at the age of 34

THE BUSINESS: A multimedia and entertainment empire, which includes TV talk shows, movies, a magazine, a radio station, and a cable channel

> "Don't be afraid. All you need to do is know who you are."
>
> — OPRAH WINFREY

We can see her on TV almost every day. She is headline news wherever she goes. Oprah Winfrey is America's most famous and influential television talk-show host. But beneath the celebrity image is a smart entrepreneur with remarkable talent.

Oprah Winfrey was incredibly successful both as a radio and a television talk-show host before she formed her own production company, Harpo Inc., in 1998. Harpo Inc. was an instant success — it produced movies for the theater and television. Its longest-running daytime television talk show, *The Oprah Winfrey Show*, is seen on national television in America and in 132 countries around the world. In 1998, Harpo's Internet company, Oprah.com went online. It became one of the top sites for her fans. That same year, Harpo co-founded Oxygen Media, which operates a cable network for women. This network reaches more than 54 million viewers. Winfrey's monthly lifestyle magazine, *O: The Oprah Magazine* overtook *Vogue*, the world's most popular fashion magazine, in circulation.

By 2007, Oprah Winfrey's personal wealth was estimated at $1.4 billion. She is the richest African-American woman in America and one of the wealthiest people in the world.

OPRAH WINFREY

GETTING THERE

Oprah Winfrey's parents were unmarried teenagers. They were both working, and she was cared for by her grandmother when she was a baby and a young child. Winfrey's love for reading came from her grandmother, who taught her how to read at a very young age. From six, she started to split her time between her mother in Milwaukee and her father in Nashville. Winfrey had a troubled youth, but she turned her life around at the age of 17 when she got a job as a part-time radio reporter in Nashville, Tennessee. At 19, she became a TV news co-anchor, the first African American in Nashville to do so. In 1976, Winfrey switched to doing talk shows. Her show became the number-one local talk show in less than a month. Her popularity led to her national TV show.

Quick Fact
Oprah Winfrey made her acting debut in the 1985 movie, *The Color Purple*. She received Academy Award and Golden Globe nominations for her performance.

THE RIGHT STUFF

From an early age, Winfrey has been driven by the will to succeed and the belief that she can. Her talk shows appeal to many because she discusses sensitive issues openly and she comes across as a warm, sincere, and caring person whom people can trust and relate to. Winfrey values her own privacy, but she will do anything to help others cope with their problems, including sharing her personal feelings and life experiences. Millions of fans watch her show daily. Her outlook and advice has become a big influence in their lives.

Quick Fact
Winfrey's success as a talk-show host did not surprise her grandmother. She noticed how smart Winfrey was as a child, and how she was "on stage" all the time, hosting talk shows with her dolls.

? Among other things, Oprah Winfrey has worked as a TV talk-show host, an actress, and a producer. In what ways do these experiences contribute to her success as a media entrepreneur? Explain.

GIVING BACK

In 1987, Winfrey created The Oprah Winfrey Foundation. Its goal is "to support the education and empowerment of women, children, and families in the United States and around the world." The charity has donated millions to improve education and health care. In 1997, Winfrey founded Oprah's Angel Network to inspire people to help others. It raised tens of millions — mostly from audience donations. In 2007, Winfrey donated $50 million to start a leadership academy for girls in South Africa.

The Expert Says...
" It is through her talk show that her influence has been greatest. When Winfrey talks, her viewers — an estimated 14 million daily in the U.S. and millions more in 132 other countries — listen. "

— Deborah Tannen, professor at Georgetown University and author of *The Argument Culture*

Danny Glover and Oprah Winfrey in Beloved, *a movie released in 1998.*

"Live Our Best Lives"

In the following quotations, Winfrey reveals her views on her life, her goals, and her success.

HER DREAMS

"The key to realizing a dream is to focus not on success but on significance — and then even the small steps and little victories along your path will take on greater meaning."

HER LIFE

"I don't think of myself as a poor, deprived ghetto girl who made good. I think of myself as somebody who from an early age knew I was responsible for myself, and I had to make good."

HER GOALS

"I think education is power. I think that being able to communicate with people is power. One of my main goals on this planet is to encourage people to empower themselves."

HER SUCCESS

"Whatever your goal, you can get there if you're willing to work."

Quick Fact
Winfrey never got the chance to go to college. But in 2007, she was honored by Howard University with a Doctorate in Humanities.

Take Note

Oprah Winfrey takes the #5 spot. An international celebrity, she is one of the most influential media people of our time. She has used her wealth to support many worthwhile causes, such as health and education in African nations. She has risen to become the foremost media person of our time and an inspiring American entrepreneur.

- Compare Oprah Winfrey with another entrepreneur that you have read about in this book. In what ways are they similar or different?

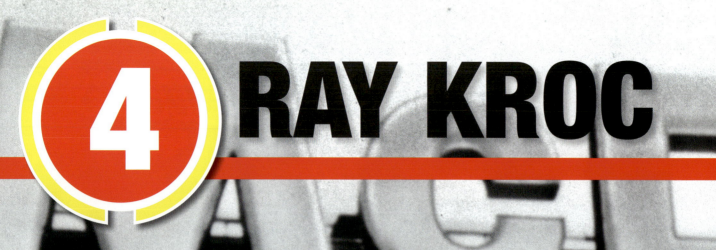

4 RAY KROC

"The definition of salesmanship is the gentle art of letting the customer have it your way."
— Ray Kroc

Ray Kroc was an ordinary person who became an extraordinary entrepreneur late in life. At the age of 52, he joined a small Californian hamburger business operated by two brothers, Dick and Mac McDonald. Kroc helped the brothers set up a chain of fast-food restaurants, which would become the world famous McDonald's with its distinctive golden arches and the McDonald clown.

Kroc did not invent the hamburger business. He created the idea of a "clean, no waiting, no surprise" eating place for people to have a quick meal. It took him many years to get his concept to work. He bought out the McDonald brothers and then reorganized the business to get things working his way. He personally organized each store to run efficiently and then sold it for a profit. This business model became the McDonald's franchising system, which has been adopted by other fast food restaurants.

McDonald's spread overseas in 1967. Kroc continued to watch over the business until his death in 1984. In that year, McDonald's sold its 50 billionth hamburger. Kroc had by then amassed a personal fortune of $500 million.

franchising: *selling the rights to operate a particular business model to another person or group*

 What influences you most when choosing a restaurant? Is it the food, price, service, location, or all of the above? Explain.

BIO: 1902–1984. Born in Chicago, Illinois; went into the hamburger business at age 52

THE BUSINESS: A fast-food restaurant chain

Ray Kroc is shown here in front of a McDonald's restaurant.

RAY KROC

GETTING THERE

Ray Kroc worked as a traveling salesperson for 30 years before he came across the McDonald brothers and their hamburger restaurant. Kroc was intrigued by how its limited menu — hamburgers, fries, and milkshakes — sped up customer choices. Kroc joined the McDonald brothers to help them set up new outlets. Eventually, the brothers sold their shares in the restaurant chain to Ray Kroc. From 1961, Kroc managed the business on his own. He set up and managed each new McDonald's outlet until it was running successfully. Then he sold each outlet for a small franchise fee, plus a percentage of restaurant sales. In addition, McDonald's owned the property on which each franchise was located and collected rent from the buyer of the franchise. This model would prove to be very profitable for Kroc.

THE RIGHT STUFF

Kroc's vision of a chain of fast food restaurants offering a simple menu, friendly service, and a clean place to have a fast meal became his passion. He trained his staff to meet the high standards he set for the business. He was a tough manager who expected his employees to work hard. He made surprise visits to check on the staff and the restaurants.

Kroc was creative in trying to please his customers. McDonald's adds new food items regularly, to satisfy changing tastes. The restaurants offer toys and games as part of its promotional campaigns.

 If you were to start a business, would you pick someone like Ray Kroc as your partner? Why or why not?

GIVING BACK

Throughout his life, Ray Kroc contributed to numerous charities. He supported the search for cures for multiple sclerosis, arthritis, and diabetes. But, by and large, Kroc left it to his wife, Joan, to do the giving. She contributed millions during her lifetime. She died in 2003, leaving $60 million to Ronald McDonald House Charities, which funds programs around the world for critically sick children and their families.

A 1948 picture of Dick and Mac McDonald's original restaurant in San Bernardino, California.

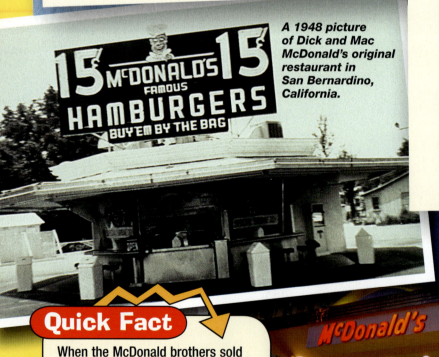

One of the most famous McDonald's restaurants in the world, Chicago's Rock and Roll McDonald's, was remodeled and reopened in 2005.

Quick Fact
When the McDonald brothers sold their business to Ray Kroc in 1961, they retained their rights to 0.5% of McDonald's franchise revenue. Owning this small percentage of the company made them very wealthy.

McDonald's by the Numbers

Ray Kroc worked long and hard to ensure the McDonald's chain lived up to his standards. This list of numbers tells the story of McDonald's success over the years.

120	The number of countries with McDonald's restaurants
1955	The year Kroc opened his first McDonald's restaurant in Des Plaines, Illinois (near Chicago)
1968	The year Big Mac was introduced in Pittsburgh by Jim Delligati
31,000	The approximate number of McDonald's restaurants worldwide by 2007
54 million	The approximate number of customers served each day (compared to 17 million in 1984)
440 million	The dollar amount of grants and donations given out by McDonald's
23 billion	The dollar amount of McDonald's yearly worldwide sales

Quick Fact
In 1963, Kroc introduced the Ronald McDonald clown. He was an instant hit with children. By 1965, the clown was familiar to 96% of American children.

The Expert Says...

" McDonald's begat an industry because a 52-year-old mixer salesman understood that we don't dine — we eat and run. "

— Jacques Pepin, French chef, author, and host of the popular PBS television series, *Jacques Pepin's Kitchen*

begat: *created*

Take Note

Ray Kroc turned a little eatery named McDonald's Hamburgers into a global phenomenon. He believed in his vision and achieved success through persistence, willpower, and leadership. He changed how the world viewed fast food and transformed the lifestyles of many generations of customers. From ordinary to extraordinary, Ray Kroc is our choice for the #4 spot on our list.
- Do you agree with our ranking of Ray Kroc? What reasons would you give to argue for or against the ranking of Ray Kroc at #4 on our list?

5 **4** 3 2 1

3 BILL GATES

In 2005, **TIME** magazine named Bill Gates one of its *Persons of the Year* for his commitment to philanthropy.

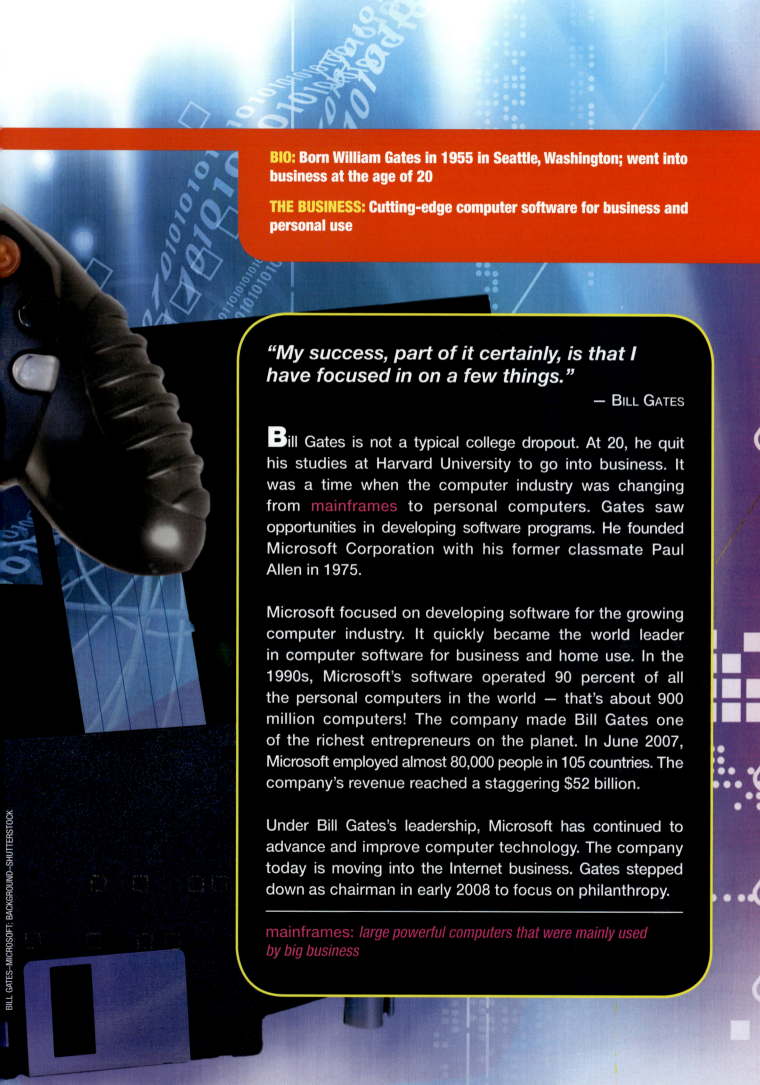

BIO: Born William Gates in 1955 in Seattle, Washington; went into business at the age of 20

THE BUSINESS: Cutting-edge computer software for business and personal use

"My success, part of it certainly, is that I have focused in on a few things."

— BILL GATES

Bill Gates is not a typical college dropout. At 20, he quit his studies at Harvard University to go into business. It was a time when the computer industry was changing from mainframes to personal computers. Gates saw opportunities in developing software programs. He founded Microsoft Corporation with his former classmate Paul Allen in 1975.

Microsoft focused on developing software for the growing computer industry. It quickly became the world leader in computer software for business and home use. In the 1990s, Microsoft's software operated 90 percent of all the personal computers in the world — that's about 900 million computers! The company made Bill Gates one of the richest entrepreneurs on the planet. In June 2007, Microsoft employed almost 80,000 people in 105 countries. The company's revenue reached a staggering $52 billion.

Under Bill Gates's leadership, Microsoft has continued to advance and improve computer technology. The company today is moving into the Internet business. Gates stepped down as chairman in early 2008 to focus on philanthropy.

mainframes: *large powerful computers that were mainly used by big business*

BILL GATES

Bill Gates (right) accepts the James C. Morgan Global Humanitarian Award from Applied Materials President and CEO Michael Splinter at the Tech Museum of San Jose, California, November 15, 2006.

GETTING THERE

Bill Gates was a computer whiz kid. By age 14, he was writing computer programs. In 1974, while still studying at Harvard University, Gates revised a computer language called BASIC to allow the Altair 8800 microcomputer to respond to a few keyboard commands. In 1975, he and partner Paul Allen formed Microsoft to adapt the language for other personal computers. In 1980, Microsoft got a big break when it was asked by IBM to develop an operating system, a program for controlling keyboard commands, for its first personal computer. Instead of starting from scratch, Gates bought an application from another company and adapted it for IBM. He named it MS-DOS. It grew to become the most popular PC operating system. Gates went on to develop Windows and Microsoft Office with word processing, math, and presentation capabilities that continue to be widely used today.

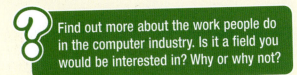

Find out more about the work people do in the computer industry. Is it a field you would be interested in? Why or why not?

THE RIGHT STUFF

Gates was hardworking and innovative. He developed one winning product after another, and went on to dominate the computer software market. He was an expert at business strategies: he was always watching his business rivals and learning from their mistakes. He hired the best brains in the computer industry and created a culture of discipline, creativity, and excellence. Microsoft became an international phenomenon in the 1990s when personal computer companies worldwide adopted the Windows operating system. Microsoft Office applications for use in the office and at home also became a huge success for Gates.

GIVING BACK

In 2000, Bill Gates and his wife Melinda started the Bill and Melinda Gates Foundation. His personal donation to the foundation has grown to over $35 billion. The foundation uses its money to develop programs that help reduce poverty and hunger in the world. It also focuses on improving health care. It offers drugs and vaccines to those in need and funds research to solve health problems. In 2007, Warren Buffet, another billionaire businessman, committed $31 billion to the Bill and Melinda Gates Foundation.

What do you think would be the challenges of managing a billion-dollar charity?

The Expert Says...

" [Bill Gates's] career delivers this message: It can be wiser to follow than to lead. ... If you hold back and follow, you can clean up in peace and quiet. "

— David Gelernter, Professor of Computer Science at Yale University

How to Give Away Billions

Bill Gates has already proven that he knows how to make billions. Now his job is to figure out how to give some of this money away. Read this article to find out what he has to say.

Bill Gates watches as his wife Melinda feeds a sick baby in Dhaka, Bangladesh.

The Bill and Melinda Gates Foundation was set up in 2000. So far, it has given out more than $14 billion to some 3,000 charities. And it still has funds of over $30 billion. Figuring out the best use for these billions is a full-time job.

In June 2006, Gates announced he would gradually give up his role at Microsoft. He explained that he has been working part-time for the Bill and Melinda Gates Foundation and full-time for Microsoft. Now he wants to reverse those priorities.

"I actually thought that it would be a little confusing during the same period of your life to be in one meeting when you're trying to make money. Then go to another meeting where you're giving it away," Gates said. He continued, "I believe with great wealth comes great responsibility. [There's the] responsibility to give back to society and make sure those resources are given back in the best possible way to those in need."

priorities: *things that are considered most important*

Quick Fact
From 1994 to 2007, the Bill and Melinda Gates Foundation committed almost $2 billion to improve education, health, and the well-being of people in the United States and other countries around the world.

Take Note
Bill Gates takes the #3 spot. His operating systems and software programs led to the widespread use of personal computers and transformed our way of life. In the process, Gates became a very wealthy man and an inspiration to other young entrepreneurs. Today, this remarkable entrepreneur is turning his attention to helping the world with the fortune he has amassed.
- How do you think Bill Gates will be remembered in history? Will it be for his impact on the computer industry, his vast fortune, or his charity work? Explain.

5　　4　　**3**　　2　　1

② HENRY FORD

With the creation of the Model T, Henry Ford revolutionized transportation in the 20th century.

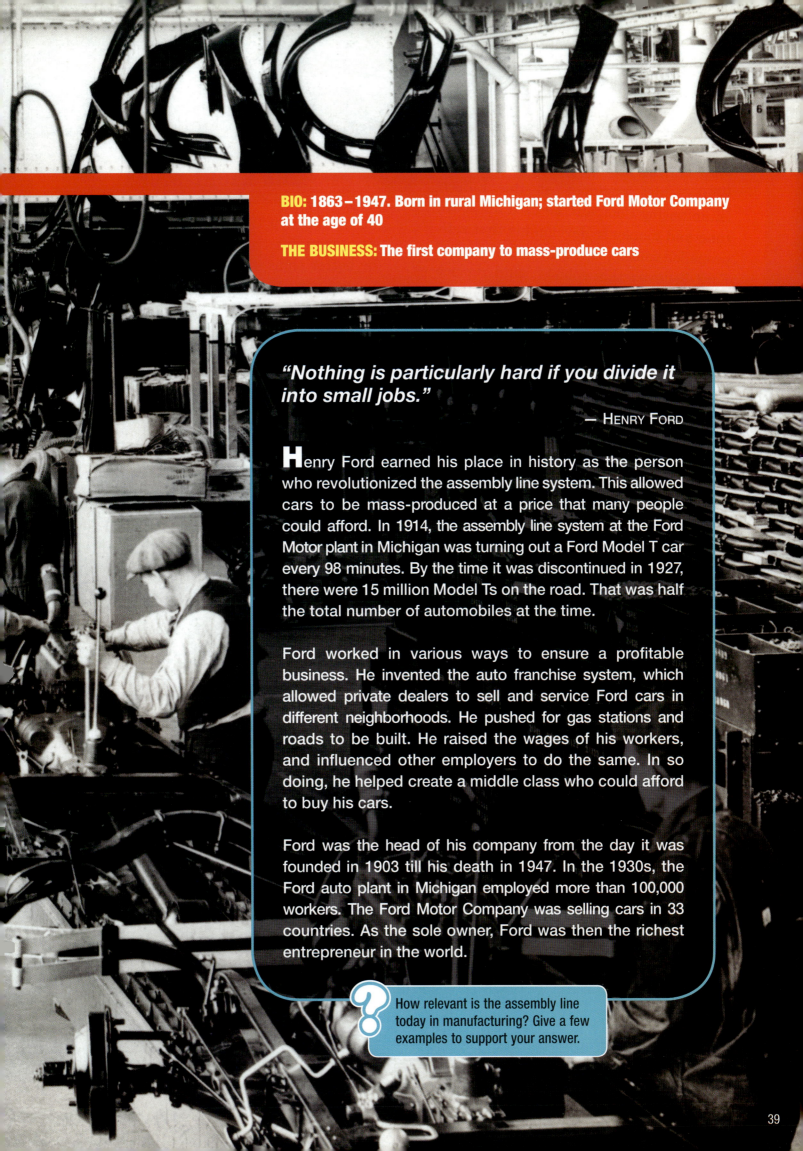

BIO: 1863–1947. Born in rural Michigan; started Ford Motor Company at the age of 40

THE BUSINESS: The first company to mass-produce cars

"Nothing is particularly hard if you divide it into small jobs."

— Henry Ford

Henry Ford earned his place in history as the person who revolutionized the assembly line system. This allowed cars to be mass-produced at a price that many people could afford. In 1914, the assembly line system at the Ford Motor plant in Michigan was turning out a Ford Model T car every 98 minutes. By the time it was discontinued in 1927, there were 15 million Model Ts on the road. That was half the total number of automobiles at the time.

Ford worked in various ways to ensure a profitable business. He invented the auto franchise system, which allowed private dealers to sell and service Ford cars in different neighborhoods. He pushed for gas stations and roads to be built. He raised the wages of his workers, and influenced other employers to do the same. In so doing, he helped create a middle class who could afford to buy his cars.

Ford was the head of his company from the day it was founded in 1903 till his death in 1947. In the 1930s, the Ford auto plant in Michigan employed more than 100,000 workers. The Ford Motor Company was selling cars in 33 countries. As the sole owner, Ford was then the richest entrepreneur in the world.

> How relevant is the assembly line today in manufacturing? Give a few examples to support your answer.

HENRY FORD

GETTING THERE

Ford started his career as a machinist. While chief engineer at the Edison Illuminating Company, he used his spare time and money to develop his first self-propelled vehicle, called the "Quadricycle." Ford believed this vehicle could replace the horse-drawn carriage. His financial backers thought differently. They saw it as a toy for the rich because it cost too much to build. So Ford started the Ford Motor Company on his own. His company invented the famous Model T in 1908. But it was still very expensive to build one car at a time. It was only around 1910 when Ford came up with the assembly line concept. In 1914, he perfected the system and revolutionized the way automobiles were manufactured.

? What are some modern cars you would consider to be playthings only for the rich?

Quick Fact
Built one at a time, the Ford Model T sold for $825 in 1908. In 1914, when the car was mass-produced under the assembly line system, it sold for $290. Even at this price, the car turned a good profit!

Quick Fact
Henry Ford was a prolific inventor. He had 161 U.S. patents in his name.

THE RIGHT STUFF

Today, it's hard to imagine life without the automobile. In 1903, people couldn't see how an expensive, breakdown-prone car could be better than a horse. Ford was not afraid to go against the thinking of his time. He was determined to bring about a world with "horseless carriages." And Ford made good business decisions. His assembly line system helped to speed up production and bring down the cost of his cars. As he reduced the price, he succeeded in selling more cars.

GIVING BACK

Henry Ford set up the Ford Foundation in 1936. It funded the Henry Ford Hospital and the Henry Ford Museum in Michigan. In the 1950s, the foundation supported the arts and humanities. In 2000, the foundation gave funds to help students from developing countries pursue higher education. Today, the foundation has assets of $12.5 billion and is one of the largest in the world. Its goals are "to strengthen democratic values, reduce poverty and injustice, promote international cooperation, and advance human achievement."

Dropping a Ford engine into the Model T in 1913

The Expert Says...

" [Henry Ford] figured that if he paid his factory workers a real living wage and produced more cars in less time for less money, everyone would buy them. "

— Lee Iacocca, President of Ford, and later Chairperson of Chrysler Corporation

Assembly Lines Through Time

Henry Ford did not invent the assembly line production system. But in 1913, he and a few talented executives unveiled his Ford Motor Company assembly line system. It was based on existing factory methods, but Ford revolutionized the way we organize work flow and production, as this report shows.

Before Ford introduced his moving assembly line system, it took time to build a product. A worker had to put all the different parts together. Production was slow, and the quality of the product depended on the skill and experience of the worker.

Ford wanted to speed up production in his manufacturing plant, so that he could build more units of his vehicle, the Model T. He and his team mapped out all the steps involved in building the vehicle. They laid out all the stages of work in a single line, from the first step to the last. They used a conveyor belt, about 240 feet long, to move the work completed at each stage to the next worker standing in line. The parts and tools required for each stage of assembly were placed at each worker's workstation. Workers had to do only one part of the assembly, and they quickly became very good at it. As a result, more cars could be built in less time, and Ford was able to lower the price of his Model T significantly.

During World War II, Henry John Kaiser used Ford's system to build ships. Kaiser's company could build a 440-foot cargo ship in just four days! After the war, more products were mass produced at lower cost using the assembly line system. This led to a dramatic improvement in the standard of living in the United States and other industrial countries in the world.

Today, computer technology can map and plan in detail all the stages in making the smallest widget or the largest structure. And robotic equipment can handle repetitive tasks with greater speed and precision.

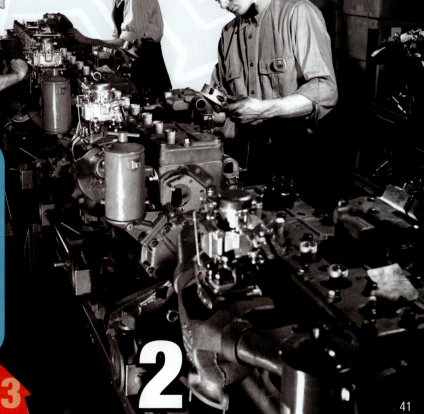

Take Note

Henry Ford drives into the #2 spot. He defied the thinking of the day and made a fortune in the process. His assembly line system helped to create the modern auto industry and the mass-manufacturing of goods. It has revolutionized the way we live.
- Do you agree that Henry Ford should rank ahead of Bill Gates? What would be your arguments for or against our ranking?

1 THOMAS ED[ISON]

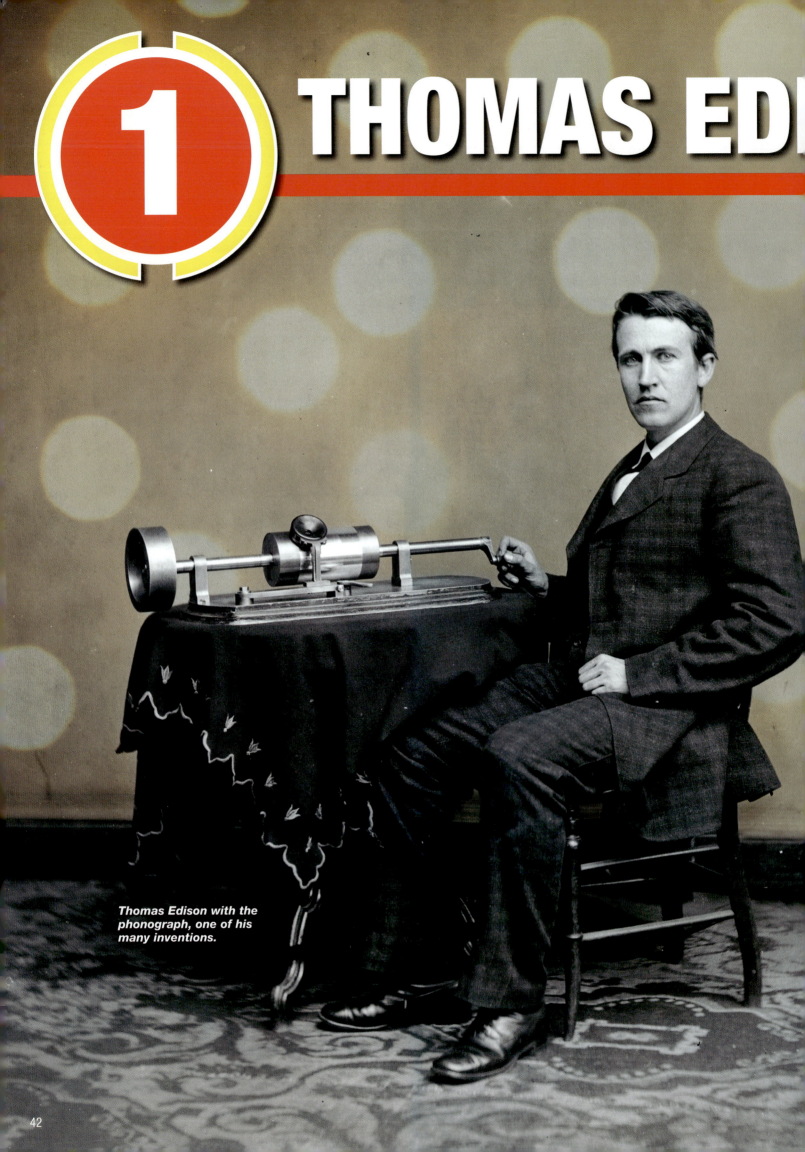

Thomas Edison with the phonograph, one of his many inventions.

SON

BIO: 1847–1931. Born in Milan, Ohio; went into business at 13; remained an entrepreneur until his death

THE BUSINESS: A business empire centered on turning inventions into marketable products

"Genius is one percent inspiration, ninety-nine percent perspiration."

— Thomas Edison

Thomas Edison was as remarkable an entrepreneur as he was an inventor. Edison patented more than 1,000 inventions in his lifetime. He used his genius to turn his inventions into products that many people could use, such as light bulbs and batteries. Edison sold his first invention for $40,000 — a sum worth many hundreds of thousands of dollars in today's money. A true entrepreneur, Edison invested all the money into building a research laboratory. It was in this lab that he came up with many great inventions that transformed our way of life.

At the time of Edison's death in 1931, there were 14 companies bearing his name. Edison's General Electric Company evolved to become today's GE, once the largest company in the world.

Unlike other entrepreneurs in this book, who left their mark in a particular business or industry, Edison's companies and business ventures dominated many industries, such as music, telecommunications, and electricity. He was one of the most successful entrepreneurs at the turn of the 20th century, and he towers above the giants of American business. He retired with a personal wealth of almost $12 million.

---

patented: *registered an invention with the government so that only he could sell it*

THOMAS EDISON

GETTING THERE

Thomas Edison only spent three months in the school system. According to his teacher, Edison was always daydreaming or asking too many questions. He was taken out of school and taught by his mother. Edison was always interested in how things worked. He loved reading technical books, and started inventing things at a young age. He started work at 12, selling candy and newspapers. By 13, he was running several businesses, including his own weekly newspaper and vegetable stand. Edison's first patent was for the electric vote recorder in 1869. His invention of the phonograph in 1877 made him famous.

> **?** What do you think would be the most difficult obstacles to overcome in introducing new products to the market?

Quick Fact
Edison lived during the Industrial Age, a time of new ideas and innovations. At first, he paid a lot of attention to what other people were developing, but over time he began to isolate himself more and more and focus only on his own ideas.

> **?** How could isolation affect an inventor and entrepreneur in a positive and negative way? Explain.

The Expert Says...
"Put simply, Edison succeeded more than other inventors of his day primarily because he was a better businessman."
— Blaine McCormick and Paul Israel, authors of *Underrated Entrepreneur: Thomas Edison's Overlooked Business Story*

THE RIGHT STUFF

Edison turned his inventions into business opportunities. He focused on creating products that were of practical value, and he patented his inventions so he could profit from them. Edison knew how to sell his ideas. He attracted investors by giving them a share of his business, but he was always the person in charge. A good leader, Edison motivated his staff and drew on their creative ideas and talents. He was extremely dedicated. He slept for only two to four hours each night. He inspired his staff to be hardworking, persistent, and flexible — qualities needed in the competitive world of product innovation.

GIVING BACK

Edison did not create any charitable foundation. There were no records regarding his contributions to charity. But he was known to be generous. Once during a tour of a Native American reservation, he installed light fixtures and put up light bulbs in all its outhouses. His inventions and the industries he created were his legacy and greatest gift to humankind.

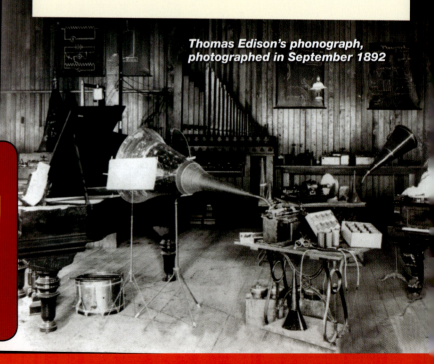

Thomas Edison's phonograph, photographed in September 1892

AMERICA'S INVENTIVE Entrepreneur

This article excerpt from *Babson Insight* describes the environment in which Thomas Edison lived and thrived as an inventor and entrepreneur.

Can you imagine life without electric lights, distributed electrical power, movies and video, and recorded sound?

Many great inventors and entrepreneurs have helped to shape the world around us, but one stands above the rest as a towering colossus for the ... impact that his life and discoveries have had on modern society ...

Even now as we look across the landscape of corporate America his impact is clearly visible. His corporate offspring and related firms rank among the largest in the world. ... General Electric was originally formed as a result of a merger of Edison's General Electric Company with another firm. ...

America during the age of Edison was a rapidly industrializing nation. ... This environment of course presented Edison with the challenge of intense competition and constant economic, technical, and social change which combined to produce great risks. The remarkable fact ... is that although many individuals invented and profited from developing new technologies, none except Edison were able to do this repetitively over his approximately 50-year career. His fame was so widespread that in 1922 a *New York Times* poll named Edison "The Greatest Living American."

Edison in his lab

Take Note

Thomas Edison is at the top of our list. He had many great ideas and the ability to recognize their business potential. Edison's research work never strayed from his objective of creating products that were saleable. He became one of the most influential entrepreneurs of his time. He had a strong business sense; he communicated his vision; and he had influence over partners, employees, and his peers.
- What might entrepreneurs today learn from Thomas Edison? Would he be a good role model for them? Why or why not?

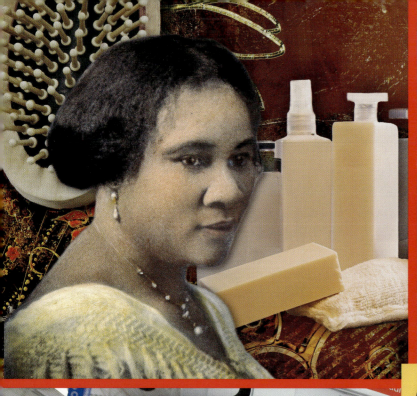
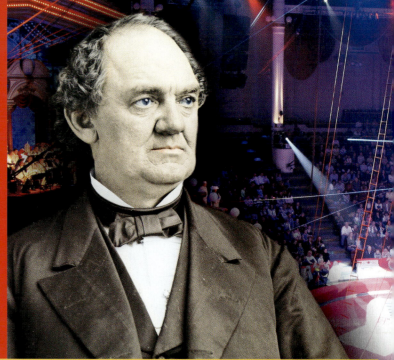

We Thought …

Here are the criteria we used in ranking the 10 most remarkable American entrepreneurs.

The entrepreneur:
- Founded an important business
- Overcame obstacles to make it to the top
- Broke new ground with his or her invention or business
- Changed the way we live
- Had global success
- Succeeded where others failed
- Is dedicated to philanthropy

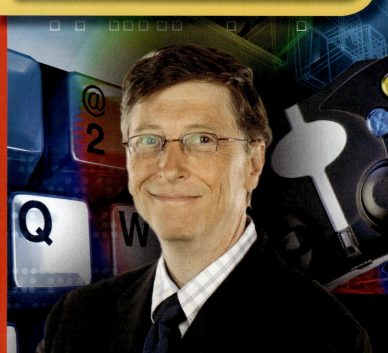

What Do You Think?

1. Do you agree with our ranking? If you don't, try ranking these entrepreneurs yourself. Justify your ranking with data from your own research and reasoning. You may refer to our criteria, or you may want to draw up your own list of criteria.

2. Here are three other remarkable American entrepreneurs that we considered but in the end did not include in our top 10 list: Walt Disney, Vera Wang, and Felix Tijerina.
   - Find out more about them. Do you think they should have made our list? Give reasons for your response.
   - Are there other remarkable American entrepreneurs that you think should have made our list? Explain your choices.

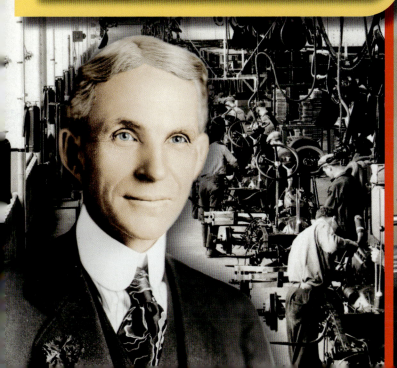

Index

A
Allen, Paul, 35–36
Arkansas, 24
Ash, Mary Kay, 14–17
Assembly line, 39–41
Autobiography of P. T. Barnum: Clerk, Merchant, Editor, and Showman, The, 13

B
Bailey, James A., 13
Barnum, P. T., 10–13
Bill and Melinda Gates Foundation, 36–37
Breedlove, Sarah, 6–7
Brin, Sergey, 18–21

C
California, 20–21, 30, 32, 36
Chicago, 31–33
China, 24–25
Colorado, 26
Connecticut, 11–12

D
Dallas, 15
Denver, 7, 26
Disney, Walt, 47

E
Edison, Thomas, 42–45

F
Ford Foundation, 40
Ford, Henry, 38–41
Ford Motor Company, 39–41

G
Gates, Bill, 34–37, 41
Gelernter, David, 36
General Electric Company, 43, 45
Glass, David, 25
Google Inc., 18–21
Google.org, 20

H
Harpo Inc., 27
Huey, John, 24

I
Iacocca, Lee, 40
Illinois, 31, 33
Indianapolis, 9
Israel, Paul, 44

K
Koehn, Nancy F., 8–9
Kotter, John P., 16
Kroc, Ray, 30–33

L
Louisiana, 7

M
Madam C. J. Walker Manufacturing Company, 9
Mary Kay Ash Charitable Foundation, 16
Mary Kay Cosmetics Inc., 15, 17
Mary Kay on People Management, 16
Mary Kay: The Story of America's Most Dynamic Businesswoman, 16
Mary Kay: You Can Have It All, 16
McCormick, Blaine, 44
McDonald's, 30–33
Michigan, 19, 39–40
Microsoft Corporation, 35–37
Milwaukee, 28
Model T, 38–41
Moscow, 19

N
Nashville, 28
New York City, 12

O
O: The Oprah Magazine, 27
Ohio, 43
Oklahoma, 23
On Her Own Ground: The Life and Times of Madam C. J. Walker, 9
Oprah.com, 27
Oprah's Angel Network, 28
Oprah Winfrey Foundation, 28
Oprah Winfrey Show, The, 27
Oxygen Media, 27

P
Page, Larry, 18–21
Patent, 40, 43–44
Pepin, Jacques, 33
Phonograph, 42, 44
Pittsburgh, 7, 33

R
Ringling Bros. and Barnum & Bailey Circus, 11–12
Ronald McDonald House Charities, 32

S
Seattle, 35

T
Tannen, Deborah, 28
Tennessee, 28
There's a Customer Born Every Minute: P.T. Barnum's Secrets to Business Success, 12
Tijerina, Felix, 47

U
Underrated Entrepreneur: Thomas Edison's Overlooked Business Story, 44
United States, 4, 9, 13, 19, 23–24, 28, 37, 41

V
Vise, David, 20
Vitale, Joe, 12

W
Wagner, Mary Kathlyn, 15
Walker, Madam C.J., 6–9, 17
Wal-Mart, 22–25
Walton Family Foundation, 24
Walton, Sam, 22–25
Wang, Vera, 47
Washington, 35
Winfrey, Oprah, 26–29